WITCHING HOUR

WITCHING HOUR

HOUR

a JOURNAL *for* CULTIVATING
POSITIVITY, CONFIDENCE,
and other MAGIC

Sarah Bartlett

Illustrated by
Rachel Urquhart

ABRAMS NOTERIE, NEW YORK

Printed and bound in China
10 9 8 7 6 5 4 3 2 1

ABRAMS The Art of Books
195 Broadway, New York, NY 10007
abramsbooks.com

ISBN 978-1-4197-3471-7

For Abrams:
Editor: Ginny Dominguez
Design Manager: Diane Shaw
Production Manager: Alison Gervais

Conceived, edited, and designed by
Quarto Publishing plc, an imprint of
The Quarto Group
6 Blundell Street
London N7 9BH

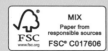

MIX
Paper from responsible sources
FSC
www.fsc.org
FSC® C017606

For Quarto:
Editor: Victoria Lyle
Senior Designer: Martina Calvio
Art Editor and Designer: Karin Skånberg
Illustrator: Rachel Urquhart
Editorial Assistant: Cassie Lawrence
Publisher: Samantha Warrington

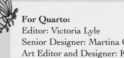

CONTENTS

HOW TO BE A WITCH
PAGE 8

CHAPTER 3
ABUNDANCE & PROSPERITY
PAGE 58

CHAPTER 4
VOCATION & LIFESTYLE
PAGE 74

CHAPTER 5
HOME & WELL-BEING
PAGE 92

CHAPTER 6
SUCCESS &
CREATIVITY
PAGE 110

CHAPTER 7
DREAMS &
GOALS
PAGE 126

CHAPTER 8
FRIENDSHIP &
MENTORS
PAGE 140

HOW TO BE A WITCH

THE WITCHING HOUR *is a guided journal for you, the modern-day witch. In fact, "the witching hour" is the time you take for reflection, spiritual work, spells, or just to focus on what you want for your future. But this is no ordinary spell book. It takes you on a journey of self-discovery and self-improvement. It enables you to be the active agent in your own life, to make your own choices, and to make things you want to happen, well, happen. This is what the witching hour's magic is all about.*

Spells and ingredients

The spells in this book require a few basic ingredients that most witchy women should have on hand. These are the tried and trusted traditional enhancements and amplifiers of the energy you are working with. Some spells include mirrors, candles, and crystals. Most importantly, you will need a pen or pencil to write in this book. A few colored pens, crayons, or paints are required, too, plus a few photos or images (depending on the spell) and other easily obtained items.

Timing

Many spells suggest working according to the lunar cycle—this is traditional witchcraft timing at its best. According to witch lore, the moon's cycle helps to manifest our

desires when it's waxing (growing bigger from new crescent moon to full moon) and helps us let go of the past or perform banishing spells when it is waning (transitioning between full moon and dark new moon).

Dos and don'ts

There are a few dos and don'ts about being a witch. Every spell or charm is done for the good of the whole universe, not just for yourself. Yes, focus on yourself for now, but never do harm to others, even if people have been backstabbing, irritating, or downright evil. Never cast your energy directly onto someone in the form of a curse, for their negativity could fall back on you. You can of course banish their bad vibes or drop old baggage and move on, but never with an intention to hurt or cause pain, even if you have been hurt and wounded yourself.

Good bewitchment is not about negativity, but about empowerment. With the right intentions, we can expect that what we ask for, we usually get. That means if you're putting out negative thoughts to the universe, you'll get negativity back; and if you're putting out positive, harmonizing energy, you'll get positivity back. Likewise, love yourself first, and others will love you, too.

BEFORE YOU BEGIN
The Witch's Oath

Before you start to work within the journal, you first need to take this oath, a promise and intention to do good. By the way, you don't have to do every spell in the order given. Your priority may be to sort your love life out, create job opportunities, or manifest a goal, but I suggest doing one of the spells in chapter one first. They focus inward and can help put you in the right spiritual, mental, and emotional state for doing further work.

The first spell starts here, though. You're simply going to cast a spell on yourself—the witch's oath. Write it out on this page, and mean it.

So this is now the Witching Hour
A time to Concentrate my Power
I only Work to do no Harm
And Focus on the perfect Charm.

SELF-WORTH & CHARISMA

CHAPTER

1

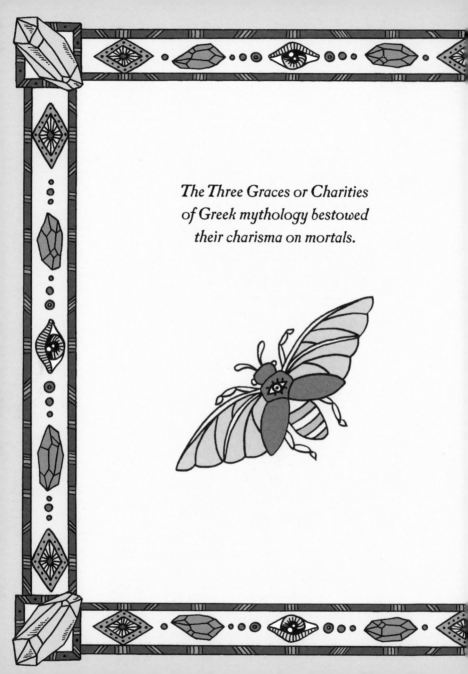

*The Three Graces or Charities
of Greek mythology bestowed
their charisma on mortals.*

We all want to radiate inner beauty, to feel good about ourselves, and to exude that mysterious quality, charisma. The word charisma originates from a Greek word meaning "divine grace." This hidden, divine aspect is in all of us, but some seem to have more than others. Unleashing your charisma is the first step to kickstarting all the other witchy things you want to happen in your life.

Starting with yourself is also the best way to get the universe to work in your favor. If you're happy with yourself—if you feel charismatic and charming, enchanting and beguiling—then the world will reflect that back at you, bringing more happiness into your life. So why not start with yourself and what you believe?

TURQUOISE

MALACHITE

ONYX

SELF-BELIEF ENCHANTMENT

Belief is everything. It shapes your life, your dreams, and your desires. Believing in the magic of yourself is the key to a positive, deliciously defined you. This enchantment works with the symbolic power of the four elements (fire, water, air, and earth) along with the fifth unknown, but most powerful, element: you.

WHAT YOU NEED

* ✿ Red candle
  (fire energy)
* ✿ Pure spring water
  in a small bowl
  (water energy)
* ✿ Red pen/pencil

This spell works best during a waxing moon. Light the candle and place the bowl of water in front of it (fire and water reflecting one another maximizes their power). Write the following words beneath each of the five crystals illustrated above with your red pen. Writing invokes air energy, and the illustrated crystals represent earth energy.

"Belief" below "Turquoise"
"Trust" below "Malachite"
"Integrity" below "Onyx"
"Compassion" below "Blue sapphire"
"Myself" below "White quartz"

BLUE SAPPHIRE   **WHITE QUARTZ**

_____   _____

Then say the following charm nine times
(an auspicious power number).

As I Believe in myself, I evolve and learn
As I Trust in my choices, I give and I earn
As I Accept others, I shape my integrity
As I Love others, I accept my own vanity
As I Believe in myself, so will it be
That whatever I have is meant just for me.

How does this spell resonate with you right now?
What self-beliefs are you cultivating?

_____

_____

_____

_____

_____

_____

CHARISMA ENHANCER

We all have charisma: It's our personal mystique and charm. Some of us seem to radiate it more easily than others, free from inhibitions or fear of what others might think. But we can all do so with the help of goddess power.

WHAT YOU NEED
- ✿ **White candle (for fire and to invoke spiritual energy)**
- ✿ **Mirror (to reflect the truth and double your power)**
- ✿ **Ribbon (optional)**

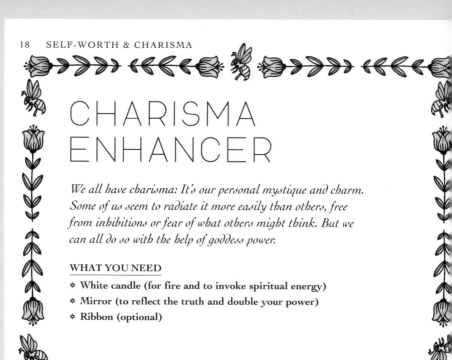

Caris is one of the Three Graces in Greek mythology. By invoking her energy, you can exude your innate "divine grace."

Wild roses are the symbolic flower of the Three Graces. Below the bouquet (opposite), write Caris's spell. Gaze at yourself in a mirror with the white candle lit and placed to the left side of your journal. Read the spell aloud three times to invoke the Three Graces' energy and to enhance your charisma wherever you go.

Now Caris comes with all her arts
To bring me gifts of each her crafts
Of grace, allure, of charm and more
My aura fills with witchy awe.

Affix a real ribbon to the bouquet or sketch a ribbon tied
in a bow around it to seal your intention.

C⊙NFIDENCE B⊙⊙STER

After centuries of being told that women should be seen and not heard, it's no wonder we sometimes struggle with self-confidence. The time has come to embrace your inner witch, sweep stereotypes aside, and learn to love yourself.

During a waxing moon, think about and write down all your good qualities on the pebbles here. Once you have finished, cover the page with your hands and say:

These stones represent all the good things in me.
May I always remember that I am unique in the universe
and possessing of the divine spark of the Old Ones.
The God and Goddess are within me; my spirit guides are around me.
I am a child of the stars and I therefore claim my right to happiness
and the unconditional love that warms the soul.
I am. I am. I am.

Every time you need a confidence boost, turn to this page and read the spell again to remind you what a wonderful person you are.

Write your best qualities on these pebbles.

ANIMAL SPIRIT GUIDE INVOCATION

Outer beauty and charisma are dependent on the state of your inner soul. To nurture the spiritual side of yourself, why not call on a spiritual guide to look after you? Animal spirit guides are invoked by shamans and witchy folks among indigenous peoples worldwide, and are totems of specific powers that you may find you are seeking in life.

WHAT YOU NEED

✤ **White candle (for fire energy, which attracts spiritual help)**

Look at the list of animals on the next page. Which attributes do you identify with right now? Choose the guide that resonates with you. Once you perform this spell, your guide will always be there to nurture your soul, so that your outer spirit glows.

Petition your chosen animal spirit guide by burning a white candle during a full moon (to maximize the effect), and repeating the following spell nine times:

My spirit guide of all I do
My soul is safe when calling you.

Sit for a while, gazing into the candlelight while you imagine your animal guide—you might even glimpse your spirit friend dancing in the flame.

Choose your animal spirit guide

☐ **HORSE** —*peaceful, sociable, wild at heart*
☐ **BUTTERFLY** —*changeable, fun, playful*
☐ **FOX** —*shrewd, clever, quick-witted*
☐ **SNAKE** —*creative, inspiring, sexual*
☐ **EAGLE** —*insightful, objective, strong*
☐ **CAT** —*magical, intuitive, independent*

☐ **TIGER** —*strong-willed, independent, astute*
☐ **OWL** —*honest, wise, capable of foresight*
☐ **WHALE** —*devoted, gentle, dependable*
☐ **SWAN** —*pure, loyal, graceful*
☐ **DOG** —*instinctive, protective, intelligent*

Sketch or find and affix an image of your spirit animal below to invoke their magical influence.

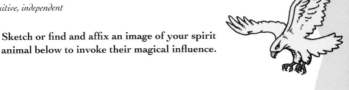

Whenever you feel the need to be in touch with your spiritual self, turn to this page, repeat the spell, and call on your animal guide.

MIRROR MAGIC

The mirror is one of the most ancient tools used for magic and divination. Its reflective power, whether by water, crystal, or looking glass, amplifies the energy of whatever is reflected. When we look at ourselves in a mirror we see our outer image, or surface beauty. But this spell will enhance and radiate your inner beauty.

WHAT YOU NEED

* ✿ **Hand-held mirror**
* ✿ **Red candle**
* ✿ **Lipstick, preferably red**

Pick up a hand-held mirror and look yourself in the eye. Spend some time thinking about all your most attractive personal qualities. If you find this difficult, think about what your best friend, partner, or family might say about you. Write these in the center of the mirror on the next page.

Call on the power of Aphrodite, the Greek goddess of love, known for her beauty, to enhance the things that you love about yourself. During a waxing moon phase (to maximize energy), light the candle, gaze at yourself in the hand-held mirror, and whisper softly:

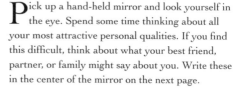

I am the fairest of them all
As Aphrodite's power is mine to call
You are my goddess who gives me light,
From now on I will shine thus bright.

Seal your intention by kissing the center of the mirror on the next page with your lipstick-reddened lips. Blow out the candle, and your true beauty will radiate wherever you go.

Write a list of your most attractive qualities.

CRYSTAL EMP⊕WERER

Crystals have unique vibrational power and enhance your self-confidence and sense of purpose. The compass rose opposite is a magical symbol that creates a connection to universal energy and amplifies the qualities of each crystal placed there. This spell will empower you with drive, strength, and motivation.

WHAT YOU NEED

* ✿ White candle
* ✿ Five clear quartz crystals (four representing the four elements and the fifth representing the quintessential energy of you)

L ight a white candle to symbolize and promote active, motivational energy.

On the next page, place a crystal to the north, to the south, to the east, to the west, then finally in the center (the crossed pathway seals the intention).

Each time you lay a crystal in place, repeat these affirmations:

> *I empower myself with confidence.*
> *I fill myself with determination.*
> *I unleash my true potential.*
> *I value all that I have and know.*
> *I invest in my future.*

If you want to further enhance your positive qualities, replace the central crystal with your birth-sign crystal (see below).

Your birth-sign crystal

☐ **ARIES** *Red carnelian*   ☐ **TAURUS** *Emerald*   ☐ **GEMINI** *Citrine*   ☐ **CANCER** *Moonstone*
☐ **LEO** *Tiger's eye*   ☐ **VIRGO** *Peridot*   ☐ **LIBRA** *Blue sapphire*   ☐ **SCORPIO** *Malachite*
☐ **SAGITTARIUS** *Turquoise*   ☐ **CAPRICORN** *Onyx*   ☐ **AQUARIUS** *Amber*   ☐ **PISCES** *Amethyst*

Take the crystals off the page, and write the first line of the charm at north, the second line at south, third line at east, fourth line at west, and fifth line in the center.

Keep the crystals in a pouch in a secret place and, if you ever feel in need of a boost of confidence, repeat the spell aloud.

FOUR WINDS MOTIVATOR

The four winds of the north, south, east, and west have long been considered powerful energies. Depending on which wind the main entrance of your home faced, you would call on the other three winds to balance the energy to create a harmonious home. This spell uses a similar method to balance your sense of purpose, drive, and motivation—too little of one wind and you feel unmotivated; too much of another and your ego could overreact.

WHAT YOU NEED

✤ **Green candle (for ambition and motivation)**

Below is a list of the qualities associated with the four winds. Decide which attribute you aspire to most right now, and write its name in the relevant cloud (e.g. "ambition" in "north wind").

North wind—Ambition
East wind—Creativity
South wind—Success
West wind—Security

Light the candle and ask all four winds to blow positive energies:

> *Personal power will be my right*
> *When the four winds blow in tonight.*

To complete the charm, write the qualities of the other three winds in the appropriate places, and draw a circle with your finger around each one to sanction your desire. You will soon be motivated to achieve whatever it is you truly want to do.

Write the attribute you desire most in the relevant cloud. Say the charm.

Add the other qualities to the other clouds. Then draw a circle with your finger around each.

NORTH *wind*

WEST *wind*

EAST *wind*

SOUTH *wind*

FREE YOURSELF FROM NEGATIVITY

In medieval white magic, wands or batons were waved around in the home to deflect bad energy. This spell banishes negativity from your life by working with the symbolic power of the magic wand. It also uses flowers, which represent harmonious growth, and the number five, which is the number of creative action.

First, write down a list of five things that you consider negative about your life. Alongside each one, draw a wand to represent banishment.

Now write a list of five things you care about, love to do, want to do, or feel good about. Draw a flower beside each one to symbolize growth, harmony, and positive energy.

Once you have made your list, repeat this spell five times and write it down in the space on the next page:

By these wands I banish all negative thought.
By these flowers I embrace all positive intentions.
I see these flowers each day within my mind's eye
To bring me goodness, grace, and all that I desire.

Five things I want to change in my life:

1 _____

2 _____

3 _____

4 _____

5 _____

Five things I value in my life:

1 _____

2 _____

3 _____

4 _____

5 _____

_____

_____

_____

_____

UNLEASH YOUR VIVACIOUS SPIRIT

It's all very well getting serious and sensible about life, money, and career, and sure, it's fabulous to want the best for ourselves and our future. But sometimes we want to let down those Rapunzel-like tresses, throw caution to the wind, turn off our serious side, and let our most carefree self take center-stage. Here's how.

On the opposite page are symbolic magical boosters for the following:

Three red rose petals —for loving yourself
A gold ring —for flirting with the world
A red candle —for lighthearted fun
A stick of cinnamon —for unleashing desire
A sunstone —for bewitching others
A silk pouch —the container: you

Draw one continuous line to connect all these items without taking your pen off the page. To help you, follow the guided diagram. You are drawing the magical "unicursal hexagram" (it's impossible to draw a hexagram in one continuous line normally as it's made up of two overlapping triangles.) This ingenious magical design connects all and enhances the ultimate unity of these ingredients and their symbolic power.

As you draw the hexagram and join the items, say:

With this pen I draw to me
All who love to let me be
Flirt or flounce, and fearless fun
Now good witching will be done

Draw one continuous line to connect all these items without taking your pen off the page. To help you, follow this guided diagram.

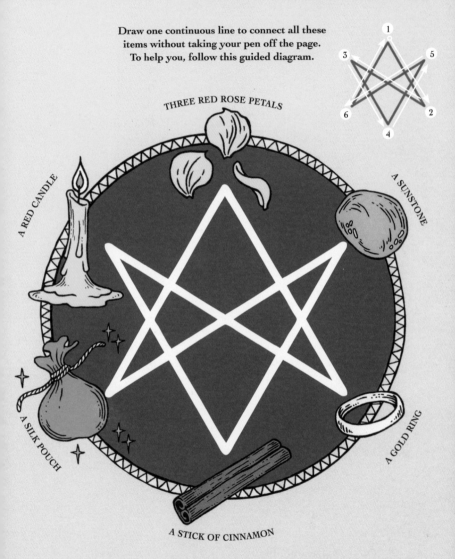

THREE RED ROSE PETALS

A SUNSTONE

A RED CANDLE

A SILK POUCH

A GOLD RING

A STICK OF CINNAMON

Now go out and flirt, flounce, and enjoy your bewitchery!

SELF-WORTH FLOWER PENTAGRAM

We all want to be loved, and we all deserve love just by virtue of being on this planet. The best place to start is by loving yourself. This spell will invoke self-value, and, in turn, will bring you the love you are looking for.

On the opposite page you'll see two pentagrams designed as flowers. The center of the image is the "seed," and the five petals are the five points of the pentagram.

In the first seed write *"I love myself."* Then write the following qualities inside each of the petal shapes: *Confidence, Gratitude, Integrity, Acceptance, Value.* Start with the top petal and work clockwise in order to amplify the potency of the charm.

To seal the spell and to be blessed with self-worth, use the second pentagram flower and write *"Myself"* in the central seed, then *"My Confidence," "My Gratitude," "My Integrity," "My Acceptance,"* and *"My Value"* in the petals, starting at the top and working clockwise.

Write the qualities inside each of the petal shapes in the five points of the pentagram.

MAKE MY WISH COME TRUE

We all say offhand things like, "I wish I were rich, I wish I could travel round the world, I wish I were successful, more beautiful, clever," and so on. But when we focus on practical, sensible wishes—for example, that our efforts on a project are recognized by our boss or for the opportunity to have a heart-to-heart conversation with a friend—they are likely to come true.

WHAT YOU NEED

* ✿ **White candle (to amplify the power of your wish to the universe)**
* ✿ **Colored pens/pencils**

Light the candle and concentrate on these images of things we traditionally wish upon—a star, a dandelion, a feather, a falling leaf. Choose one item, color it in, and write your wish beside it. Then complete your intention by repeating the spell aloud three times:

> *I wish for love for all around.*
> *I wish for all to be unbound.*
> *I wish for all who wish their wishes too.*
> *I wish my wish to come to me so true.*

Lastly write, "So may it be" beneath your chosen wish.

This spell is ultra-powerful because of the repetitive sounds the words make when read aloud. Remember, spells are magical because every word we speak has magical value.

Choose one item, color it in, and
write your wish beside it. There is
space for four wishes here.

Now look forward to your wish coming true.

LOVE & ROMANCE

CHAPTER

2

To get hit by Cupid's arrow is one thing, but to fire a few arrows requires courage and determination.

For centuries, witches have been asked for remedies for broken hearts, spells to attract new lovers, curses for rivals, charms to discover infidelity, cures for infertility, and, of course, spells to seal a bond forever.

This section helps you steer your love life in the direction you want it to take. It's not about being desperate, but having a witchy desideratum. In other words, it's about knowing what you desire and lack, and what will enrich your relationship world. Are you looking for the early texts of romance to turn into a major love letter, or do you want to take control of your love destiny? Whatever you want from love, you can find it here.

TO ATTRACT NEW R⊙MANCE

Cinnamon has traditionally been used by witches to promote lust, not only because of its symbolic association with heat, but also for its power to invoke desire in another.

WHAT YOU NEED

✿ **Cinnamon powder**

Get some cinnamon powder and sprinkle it in your shoes before you go out on the town to stir romance in someone's heart.

Before you leave the house, petition your desire to the Greek goddess of love, Aphrodite, using the following knot spell to ensure you attract the right kind of attention.

Knot spells seal our intentions. Write the following charm on the pink ribbon shown here; when you get to each of the three knots of the ribbon, say the spell aloud.

Aphrodite, carry love upon the wind,
With this first knot sure to bring.

Aphrodite, let this love be true,
By my desire a knotted two.

Aphrodite, bring new love to me,
Bring it with this knotted three.

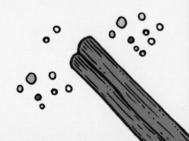

MAKE THEM SWOON SPELL

You've met your new crush and they've been drawn to you. Now let's help them fall head over heels for you (as long as you are equally crazy about them)! Swooning is a lovely word for being overcome with delight. Let's make that first date swoon over you.

WHAT YOU NEED

✽ **Garnet (either a stone, a piece of jewelry, or the illustration below)**

Garnets have been used throughout history to both repel evil and attract love. The red color of garnet symbolizes a strong love or romantic connection. It carries the energies of passion and desire.

To get that first date to swoon, empower a piece of garnet (either a stone, a piece of jewelry, or the illustration below) with the following spell. Then take the charmed object on your date with you.

Place the garnet you've chosen in the middle of the magic circle on the next page, and write the following spell around the edge to activate your garnet.

Swooning soon this date will be
This garnet brings their heart to me.

Carry your garnet with you, and your love interest will find you irresistible.

Write the spell around the edge, and your garnet will be ready and activated.

GETTING CLOSER SPELL

It's all very well dating, romancing, and getting into a relationship, but then what? Most of us want it to go somewhere. This spell will ensure that the one you adore will want to get closer to you. Whether close means a warm embrace or staying up all night sharing secrets, togetherness will be certain.

The four main compass directions are used in magical traditions because they are instilled with the power of invisible, universal energy, or what the Chinese mystics called "ch'i." Drawing on the four main directions, this spell will attract positive, binding energy to your relationship.

Write your name in red in the top half of one of the white strips on the next page, and your partner's in blue in the top half of the other. Cut them out and stick yours on the vertical axis (north to south), and your partner's on the horizontal axis (west to east).

To bind the spell and promote togetherness, write your name in blue underneath your partner's, and your partner's name in red underneath yours.

WHAT YOU NEED

* ✿ Red pen/pencil
  (red enhances passion
  and sexual affinity)
* ✿ Blue pen/pencil (blue
  promotes spiritual affinity)
* ✿ Scissors
* ✿ Clear tape/glue

Write your name in red on one of the white strips and your partner's name in blue on the other. Cut them out and stick yours on the vertical axis and your partner's on the horizontal axis. Then write your name in blue underneath your partner's name, and your partner's name in red underneath yours.

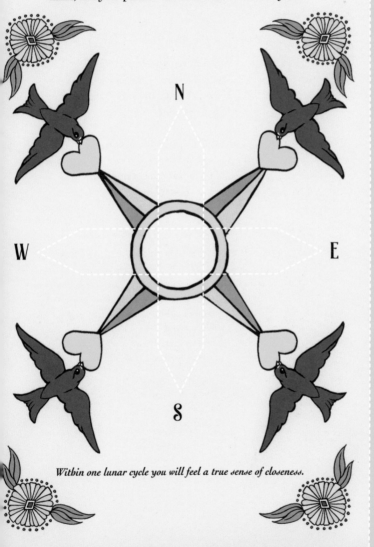

N

W

E

S

Within one lunar cycle you will feel a true sense of closeness.

BEWITCHMENT FOR SENSUAL AFFINITY

For perfect bliss between the sheets—or on top of them—cast the following spell on a full moon night to maximize the lunar power and draw down the seductive influence of the Greek goddess of love, Aphrodite.

WHAT YOU NEED

✿ **Piece of rose quartz (the crystal of love) or a cut stem rose (the flower of Aphrodite)**

Place your crystal or rose on the illustration of Aphrodite and then write the following enchantment beneath it:

By all that's lit in lunar light,
Make our love be rich each night.
With rose and silver moon we see,
Aphrodite's power for us will be.

Leave your book open with the rose or crystal exposed in a full moonlight for one night, and you'll be ready to experience perfect sensual harmony with your lover.

LOYALTY LOVE KNOT

When we bolt a padlock to a bridge railing and throw the key in the river, we're saying that we've committed to our partner forever. In the same way, a knotting spell will lock you and your partner's intention to be faithful, loyal, and true to each other.

WHAT YOU NEED

✿ **Lock of your hair**

✿ **Lock of your partner's hair, taken with their permission (or anything they have recently been in contact with that you can place inside the book, e.g. a napkin, a letter, a dollar bill)**

✿ **Double-sided sticky tape**

Place your hair and your partner's item in the middle of the Celtic love knot (a symbol of eternal fidelity) and then write the following spell beneath it. Say it aloud as you do so to promote mutual loyalty.

> *With this knot you love me, love.*
> *With this knot I love you, love.*
> *With this lock I bind our love.*
> *A love-lock of our loyalty.*

Attach here

Say the spell aloud as you write it down to promote mutual loyalty.

THEY L♥VE ME, THEY L♥VE ME NOT DIVINATION

As a kid we've all picked a daisy and pulled the petals off to divine whether someone loved us or not. The daisy is a symbol of true love and, if you look closely, you will discover that it is two flowers blended together as one.

Draw a series of daisies in the center of the magic circle on the opposite page. Repeat the flower pattern over and over again, until you fill the magic circle to seal your intention.

Write "they love me, they love me not" around the outside of the circle until you have joined the beginning to the end.

Close your eyes and move your finger around the magic circle, both clockwise and counterclockwise. When you feel the moment is right, stop moving your hand and open your eyes—whichever line your finger falls closest to will tell you the truth of your lover's current feelings. Remember though, this can change with time, so don't get downhearted if it's not the answer you were hoping for—try again tomorrow.

Draw a series of daisies in the center of the magic circle.

Write "they love me, they love me not" around the outside of
the circle. Close your eyes, move your finger around the circle,
stop when you feel the moment is right, and discover your
lover's current feelings.

MANIFESTING
AN IDEAL MATE

Sometimes we have a powerful image of what our "ideal mate" is like—what they look like, what they value, what they do for a living, and so on.

WHAT YOU NEED

* ❀ White candle
* ❀ Scissors
* ❀ Clear tape/glue

Harness your inner vision and use this simple bewitchment to manifest that someone special. This spell is not about attracting a specific individual, but a type of person—a character who fits your ideals and values. If you truly believe in this character and in this spell, then they will come into your life.

Write down the qualities you are looking for:

Looks ______________________________

Voice ______________________________

Work style ______________________________

Character ______________________________

Quirks ______________________________

Humor ______________________________

Lifestyle ______________________________

Any other "must have" characteristics—
e.g., enterprising, genuine smile, sociable, etc.

____

____

____

____

____

Once you have written your list, burn the candle for two minutes while you repeat your list over and over again. Cut out the strip on the side of the page, wrap it around your wrist, and stick the two ends together to form a bracelet. Wear this between a new moon and a full moon to manifest your perfect partner.

MANIFESTING MY
IDEAL MATE

DUMPING BAGGAGE CHARM

Sometimes we have to let go of the past, dump our personal baggage, and move on. This enchantment will release you from anything you wish to leave behind, and allow you to move forward with someone new or simply to start anew on your own. Perform this spell during a waning moon phase—between a full moon and a new moon—when the energy is aligned with releasing others and letting go.

WHAT YOU NEED

✱ **Green candle (to amplify acceptance of letting go)**

D raw a circle around each of the five illustrated crystals. Light your candle and gaze at the crystals one by one, while you focus on the qualities detailed on the label. Then draw a knot or a bow on each circle—this represents completion. As you do so, say each time:

All that must be gone from me,
be banished, and so mote it be.

Draw a circle around each of the five crystal images. Then draw a knot or bow on each circle.

ONYX
Acceptance

WHITE QUARTZ
New beginning

MALACHITE
Letting go

CITRINE
Moving on

ROSE QUARTZ
Self-love

What baggage would you like to remove right now?

You will soon discover that you are no longer a prisoner to your past, and are free to move forward.

ABUNDANCE & PROSPERITY

CHAPTER

3

*Abundance derives from a Latin word
meaning "overflowing."*

We all desire abundance in our lives. But what do we want abundance of and how much of it would we like? Abundance requires measurement. You want more money—well, how much is more? You want abundant energy, but how much energy?

You might wish for an abundance of peace, generosity, or acceptance. Whatever form of abundance you crave, measure how much you want before you do these spells.

For example, with a petition like, "I want more money," you need to say specifically, "I want $5,000 in the next six months." Being precise tells the universe what you want, so that it can help you get it!

PRØSPERITY ENCHANTMENT

During the Renaissance, astrologer and magician Cornelius Agrippa developed sixteen mystical symbols from an ancient form of divination called "geomancy." Geomancy was the art of interpreting patterns made in the earth or sand by natural forces. Each pattern is represented by a magical symbol, and each magical symbol is imbued with earth magic.

WHAT YOU NEED
✿ **Colored pens/pencils**

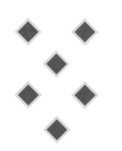

The acquisto figure is the symbol of good luck and a magical device for attracting financial prosperity. It is shown to the right.

Color the symbol for acquisito on the opposite page. Above the symbol, write your name and, in a few words, exactly how prosperous you want to be. Beneath the base of the symbol, write:

With gratitude

Meditate on this symbol for a few minutes every day, and repeat to yourself:

*I offer gratitude to the universe
and will be as prosperous as I desire to be.*

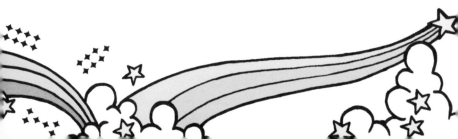

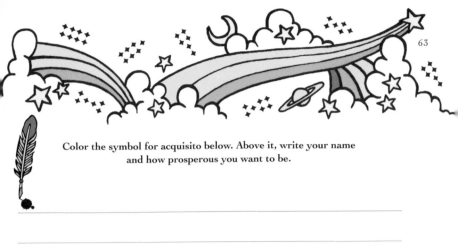

Color the symbol for acquisito below. Above it, write your name and how prosperous you want to be.

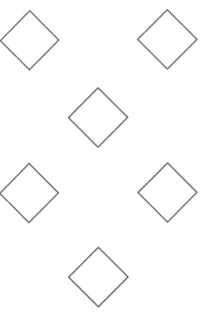

Below the symbol, write "with gratitude."

OVERCOMING OBSTACLES

Apart from financial wealth, there's also prosperity of mind, body, and spirit. Often, on our path to serenity, there are obstacles in the way. The map opposite shows an island fraught with dangers. This spell will allow you to overcome any hurdles or problems so you can reach your treasure—good fortune and well-being.

On the illustrated island is a point of departure (where the ship is docked) and a treasure chest. There are also five dangers (symbolic of the four elements and the mystical fifth element):

- Deep lakes
- Parched desert
- Terrifying scorpion
- High mountain range
- Erupting volcano

Start at the ship and draw a line that crosses the island, passing through each danger. At each danger zone, write down a word that sums up an obstacle in your life.

Once you have made your way to the chest, write down the treasure that will truly make you feel prosperous in mind, body, and spirit.

Once you have cast this magic island spell, all obstacles will be overcome on your way to prosperity.

Draw a line from the ship to the treasure, traversing each of the five dangers.

F⊕RTUNE SPELL

Good fortune can come to us in many ways, big and small. But if you want to manifest good fortune in your life, then you can try calling on the ancient Greek goddess, Tyche. The daughter of Aphrodite and Zeus, Tyche was also thought to be the goddess who governed fate. She often appeared in medieval art carrying or residing above the wheel of fortune.

WHAT YOU NEED

* ✿ White candle (for the power of the goddess)
* ✿ Red candle (for your desire)
* ✿ Yellow candle (for luck)
* ✿ Black candle (to protect and ground you)

Light the candles in the following order on the evening of a waxing moon: the white candle to the north of your journal, the red candle to the west, the yellow candle to the east, and the black candle behind you on a safe ledge or table. Read aloud this spell to Tyche. To sanction your petition to the goddess, blow the candles out one by one in the order you lit them.

> *Tyche bring me good luck true,*
> *Across my pathway good fortune too.*
> *The wheel it turns, my destiny's mine,*
> *So Tyche bring me all that's fine.*

What is your intention with this spell? In which areas of your life are you looking for luck?

Very soon, good fortune will come your way.

MANIFESTING A MAGNIFICENT LIFESTYLE

In magical circles, we say that "what goes around comes around, and sometimes tenfold." If we boldly visualize and truly believe in what will make us happy, fulfilled, or content, then it will come to us. The universe gives back to us what we put out—this is the art of manifesting our desires.

WHAT YOU NEED

* ✿ Colored pens/pencils
* ✿ Images
* ✿ Clear tape/glue

Different things make different people happy— whether it's more fun, a good job, a lovely family, or spiritual peace.

Sit quietly for a minimum of twenty minutes and contemplate the things that make *you* happy—try to visualize them in your mind as clearly as you can, being as specific as possible.

Then either sketch or find images of the things that make you smile and stick them on the opposite page. Fill the page, like a collage. It might take you a couple of evenings to do this, but the more you invest in your happiness, the more you will receive happiness from the universe.

LUNAR PLANTING

Perform this spell to draw any kind of abundance to you.
Be specific in what you wish to grow in your life.

Planting is a symbol of intention for growth. This spell calls for a symbolic planting of the following items during one lunar cycle: acorns for growth, coins for abundance, and crystals for protection.

The illustrations on the next page show five phases of the moon. Starting with the waning moon, write the following charm on each of the lunar phases during the period in question.

Waning moon:
I plant smoky quartz to let go of wastefulness.

New moon:
I plant black tourmaline to protect my interests.

Waxing moon:
I plant this acorn to root my desires.

First quarter moon:
I plant a coin to augment my wishes.

Full moon:
I plant two coins to bring abundance quickly to me.

Like all seeds, this spell may not bring immediate results.
However, do not make the mistake of thinking nothing is happening.
Eventually, green shoots will appear.

Write the charm in the cloud beneath each of the lunar phases during the period in question.

WANING MOON

NEW MOON

WAXING MOON

FIRST QUARTER MOON

FULL MOON

SOLAR MONEY ATTRACTION

Solar energy has long been associated with kings, riches, glamour, fame, gold, diamonds, and big money. This simple spell will attract money to you. It may not happen overnight, but taking the charged sunstone with you wherever you go will enhance all possible money-making opportunities you might encounter.

WHAT YOU NEED

- **Piece of sunstone to carry in a pouch or worn as jewelry**

Write each line of the spell in one of the seven rays of the sun. To activate the sunstone's money-attracting power, place it in the center of the sun, put your hands around it, and repeat the spell aloud seven times. From now on, carry the stone or wear it wherever you go.

A solar gift lies in this stone,
Of seven rays and seven thrones,
Of seven nights and seven days,
Of seven lines and seven ways,
Of seven powers and seven riches,
Of seven gods and seven witches,
Who dance the light to me.

Write each line of the spell in
one of the seven rays of the sun.

VOCATION & LIFESTYLE

CHAPTER

Abundance and prosperity are one thing,
but wise witches know how important
a sense of vocation is.

Not sure which path to go down when you reach one of life's crossroads? Before you make that kind of decision, it's essential to know what truly gives you meaning, passion, and a sense of purpose.

Some of us may be forced into career pathways by parents, family, or academic results, but a vocation is something that calls to you. It may elude you for many years, but it will keep calling until you realize there is something missing in your life and start to pursue it. If you don't feel it yet, then encourage the calling— the divine spark in yourself—to come to you.

These spells will help bring the lifestyle or sense of vocation you are looking for to you.

STARTING AFRESH SPELL

When you arrive at a crossroads in your life, you may need to banish the past before you can move on. By symbolically leaving the past behind, you can fearlessly take the next step on your journey.

WHAT YOU NEED

* ✿ **Gold candle**
* ✿ **Silver candle**

In the world of magic, you are a channel between the past and the future. The you that is in the present needs to be protected from any negativity in your past so you can start afresh.

Walk in a clockwise circle with your writing hand outstretched to create a magic circle around you.

As you do so, say the spell:

I cast this magic circle to be safe between two worlds.
I let go of the past and all that has been had.
Bring me only grace and all that is glad.
I start afresh, a new pathway.

Light a gold candle and a silver candle to amplify your request to the universe. Reflect on your future pathway for a few minutes, then blow out the candles.

Jot down your thoughts after doing this spell. What are you leaving behind? Where are you going?

EYE OF HORUS
PROTECTION

The Eye of Horus is an ancient Egyptian protective talisman. Originally associated with the snake goddess, Wadjet—the protector of kings, Egypt, and women in childbirth—in later Egyptian myth-cycles it became associated with the sky god, Horus.

WHAT YOU NEED

✵ **Red candle**

✵ **Three pieces of tiger's eye crystal or three gold rings (to symbolize and boost positive energy)**

If you are going through a period of transition, determined to change your lifestyle, or simply want to carry on enjoying your life as it is, this charm will protect you from negativity.

Light the candle, and place the three items in the center of the eye on the opposite page. Write this charm around the eye.

> *With this Eye my sight is true and clear.*
> *With this Eye my mind it has no fear.*
> *With this Eye I'm safe in every way.*
> *With this Eye I'm vitalized every day.*

Remove one crystal/ring at a time, repeating the charm as you do so. Seal the charm by dripping a drop of the red candle wax onto the Eye of Horus before you blow out the candle. Let the wax cool and set before you close the book!

Write the charm around the eye.

V⊕CATI⊕NAL DIRECTI⊕N SPELL

Each celestial body in astrological magic is associated with certain careers or vocations.

From the list below, choose the one that you consider closest to your vocational dream, and draw its symbol in the center of the circle illustrated on the next page.

WHAT YOU NEED

✻ **Colored pens/ pencils**

♂	Mars	Entrepreneur or company boss
♀	Venus	Fashion designer or beautician
☿	Mercury	Journalist or linguist
☽	The Moon	Nurse or chef
☉	The Sun	TV presenter or teacher
♃	Jupiter	Travel writer or park ranger
♄	Saturn	Real-estate broker or interior designer
♅	Uranus	Scientist or computer programmer
♆	Neptune	Psychic healer or musician
♇	Pluto	Psychotherapist or spy

Now read the spell aloud:

My vocation is fixed, my intention true,
To bring me success in all I do.
This is my calling, so bless me too.

Color the symbol of your choice with whatever color you think represents you or your future vocation while you focus on that particular pathway.

Draw and color your chosen symbol in the center of the circle.

Describe your dream vocation here:

_____

_____

_____

_____

_____

From now on you will attract positive influences to help you fulfill your vocational choice.

PRIORITY SORTING SPELL

The magical figure shown on the next page is known as tristitia in medieval magical geomancy. Though this symbol can be associated with sadness, it also signifies stability. It represents staking something to the ground, pinning your priorities down, and gaining strength.

Think about the three things you most need in your life right now. Assign each of your desires to either the acorn, sun, or butterfly symbols on the next page. Connect each pair of symbols with a gold line. Gold symbolizes growth and the ability to analyze a situation rather than merely react to it.

As you draw the first line say:
My first priority is . . .

As you draw the second line say:
My second priority is . . .

As you draw the third line say:
My third priority is . . .

Write your priorities above the gold lines.

WHAT YOU NEED

✣ **Gold pen**

Choose one of the symbols below to represent each of your
three priorities. Draw a gold line between them and write your
priorities above the lines.

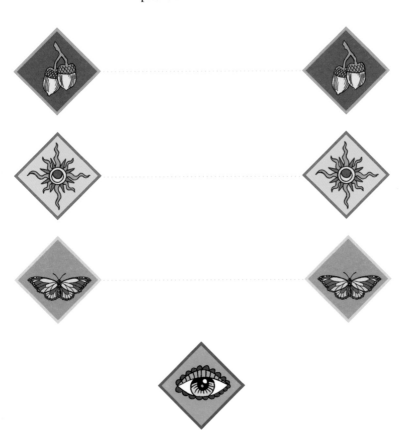

You have now staked your priorities to the ground.
You can move forward with new focus and clarity.

MY DREAM LIFESTYLE

We all dream of a certain kind of lifestyle. You might wish to travel the world carefree, to be an eternal student, or to have a great home and start a family. Whatever your dream, begin by visualizing it now. Once you start this process, it will begin to materialize before your eyes.

WHAT YOU NEED

✿ **Images**
✿ **Clear tape/glue**

Create your own mood board on the opposite page. First decide what kind of lifestyle you really want and begin to collect various images that represent that lifestyle. Choose images of luxury items if you want a lush lifestyle; pluck a blade of grass or attach a pressed leaf if you want a back-to-nature lifestyle; use photos of lakes, snow, and wildlife if you want to roam the world; and so on. Stick images around the center, then, halfway through your mood board, write the spell in the space given. Now stick more images around the spell to seal the intention. Recite the spell aloud every full moon until your lifestyle changes to the one you truly desire.

My intention is true to my dreams and desires,
And so it will come through these magical powers.
The universe brings me the life that I choose,
So that I will know I have nothing to lose,
Only to gain and bring me the light,
To see dreams becoming the lifestyle so bright.

ENHANCE THE BEST OF WHO YOU ARE

To perform this spell, first you need to decide what it is about yourself that you want to enhance. Do you want to be more spiritual, more experienced in worldly affairs, or more sure of yourself? Think of your best traits — which do you want to improve or maximize?

WHAT YOU NEED

✿ **Red pen/pencil (to enhance fire energy and augment your desire)**

Once you have decided what you want to enhance, hold this trait in your mind as you perform this knotting spell. Knotting spells are highly empowering, active spells that focus vision and seal intention.

Write out each line from this spell along a segment of the illustrated golden ribbon. When you get to a knot, say the line aloud.

With knot one, desire be done.
With knot two, my life be true.
With knot three, my choice be freed.
With knot four, I open the door.
With knot five, I come alive.
With knot six, my goal is fixed.
With knot seven my mind is driven.
With knot eight, my pathway's straight.
With knot nine, I now can shine.

FINDING THE RIGHT PATHWAY SPELL

Sometimes we just don't know where we are going in life, or what road to take. If we don't know who we really are or what our true potential is, when we reach a crossroads, how can we know which direction to take? This spell will help you discover what really matters to you in your life.

WHAT YOU NEED

✱ **Photo or picture of yourself**

The tarot card illustrated here is the World. This card symbolizes complete fulfillment and a sense of feeling on top of the world, and knowing exactly where you are going and why. This card enhances choices, pathways, and your future.

Paste a photo of yourself over the tarot card. As you do say:

> *As the sun shines on me the world brings me joy.*
> *As the full moon comes I will know my pathway.*
> *As the world turns, so will I take the right road.*
> *As the universe speaks, I will know myself.*

Write the spell beneath the image of the World, and by the next full moon you will discover what your life pathway truly is.

HOME & WELL-BEING

CHAPTER

5

With spells for home and family protection, you can relax and enjoy a better family life and improve those relationships that you may feel are not as beneficial to you right now as you would like.

Our home is where we need to feel the most safe and secure. All the spells in this section are for the protection of your environment, your family, and also your own psychic self. Your well-being depends on the interaction between your inner psychological and psychic state and your surroundings—with the right balance between you and your home, you will find your holistic well-being improves.

Also included is some feng shui, which is the ancient Chinese art of creating harmony in one's environment. It is a powerful energy for aligning you with your home, your desires, and the world around you.

HARM⊕NY IN THE H⊕ME SPELL

The four elements in western alchemical traditions are fire, earth, air, and water. Their symbols are shown below. When we want to create balanced, positive energy in the home, we can call on these elements to create harmony around us.

WHAT YOU NEED

✴ **Four candles: yellow for air, blue for water, red for fire, green for earth**

Air

Water

Fire

Earth

First, take this journal with you into every room in the home and stand quietly in the center of the room. Look at the illustrated symbols, and draw the shape of each element in the air, casting a spell on the room itself, bringing it alive with the symbolic resonance.

Light the four candles and place them on a table in the shape of a square.

Copy the elemental symbols in the diagram on the next page in this order: to the north, water; to the south, fire; to the east, air; to the west, earth.

Then write this spell in the lines below the diagram:

I bring harmony to every corner of my home,
The elements of fire, earth, air, and water are done.

Finally, blow out the candles to amplify and disperse the positive energy to all areas of your home.

Copy the elemental symbols into the diagram below in this order: to the north, water; to the south, fire; to the east, air; to the west, earth.

MAGIC NUMBER SQUARE FOR NURTURING

The ancient Taoist god of good fortune, Tian guan, was said to have been born on the fifteenth day of the first lunar month of the Chinese calendar. The Lantern Festival, marking this day, is still celebrated to honor the god, establish happy reunions, and bring the whole family luck. In this magic square, the numbers in each line add up to fifteen, whether horizontally, vertically, or diagonally, sealing the intention of the fifteenth lunar day to enhance good fortune for all the names written in the square.

Spell out the names of you and your household in the boxes on the next page. The first letter of your name goes in the box with the 1, the next letter goes in the box with the 2, and so on. When your name is complete, start the next name in the box with the next consecutive number. If you fill all nine boxes, start the next letter back in box 1.

For example, if your name is Jane, your partner is John, and your daughter is Ella, the first letter of your name is J, so write J beside the number 1. Then go to 2 and write A, then at 3, write N, at 4 write E. Then the J of John at 5, O at 6, H at 7, N at 8, E of Ella at 9, L at 1, next to your J, L at 2, next to your A, and A at 3, next to your N.

Once you have filled in the magic square, say the names of each family member fifteen times to bring the magic of the god of good fortune into your life.

Place the letters of each
family member's name in
the magic box.

4	9	2
3	5	7
8	1	6

*Once you have placed all the names in the square, seal your intention
for family protection by doodling around the square and thanking
the universe for its blessing.*

ANCESTRAL PSYCHIC PROTECTION

For thousands of years, different cultures and civilizations have prayed to their ancestors to protect them. This simple exercise, drawing down the power of your ancestral spirits, is the perfect way to ensure your family's well-being is protected.

WHAT YOU NEED

* ✽ **Photo of ancestor**
* ✽ **White candle**
* ✽ **Clear tape/glue**
* ✽ **Piece of black obsidian**

First, find a photo of an ancestor who has passed—someone you really liked, admired, or respected in some way. You only need one empowering ancestor for spiritual protection, but you can use as many as you like to strengthen your protective power.

On a full moon night, light a white candle to enhance your home with spiritual energy. Then stick the photo on the opposite page and write the name of your ancestor beneath the photo. After the name write:

I bless you [name of ancestor], both your spirit and soul.

At the bottom of the page, write:

Please bless my spirit and soul too, and protect me from all negativity wherever I go.

Place the piece of black obsidian on the photo overnight to charge the stone with their protective power. Then carry or wear the stone with you wherever you go for complete psychic protection.

Attach a photo of your ancestor below. Write their name and the ancestral blessing beneath the picture. Write the request at the bottom of the page.

Attach
photo
here

TREE OF LIFE

The Tree of Life is a well-known symbol of growth, well-being, and prosperity in many different traditions. For example, in Celtic mythology the tree was known as "Crann Bethadh" and connected the divine world to the earthly one. In Norse mythology, "Yggdrasil" was the magical tree that connected the nine planes of existence. In every culture, the Tree of Life supports and gives the power of life, well-being, and happiness.

In the image on the next page you'll see nine empty leaves on the Tree of Life. In each leaf, write a word or short sentence that describes what makes you happy. It can be spiritual, emotional, physical, or mental. Think of this as both an act of gratitude and of request. Color the leaves and then write the spell below:

WHAT YOU NEED

* Colored pens/
  pencils

My well-being and happiness grow with the branches of this tree.
My goals and intentions are safe with the roots of this tree.
I will fulfill all that I set out to do.
So mote it be.

Fill in the leaves with words that describe what makes you happy.
Color the leaves.

MAGIC MIRROR CHARM

Polished natural surfaces, like obsidian, bronze, or silver, have long been used as divining mirrors in occult circles. The mirror, of course, does not necessarily reflect the truth, but it does enhance all that it reflects. In witchy work, it amplifies the power of spells and charges whatever it reflects with its power. This spell uses a mirror to reflect and bring positive energy into your home to improve all forms of family relationships.

WHAT YOU NEED

✿ **Hand-held mirror**

First charge your mirror with the power of solar energy by leaving it in a shaded place on or near a window-ledge from dawn to dusk. DO NOT place it in direct sunlight, as this can cause scorch marks or even fire damage or hurt someone's eyes if they look into it.

In the evening, at your witching hour, place the charged mirror face down on the image of the sun opposite. Then recite the spell:

My solar light will now shine bright,
to bring me joy and pure delight.
For all my family, let love come in,
For best intentions now to win.

Take your mirror and walk through every room of your home, reflecting the corners, walls, doors—everything you walk past—to imbue the house with solar energy and to bring well-being and good intentions to everyone who lives there.

Write down the names of the members of your household
here along with a positive thought about each one.

_____

_____

_____

_____

_____

MY FAMILIAR PROTECTION CHARM

A familiar is a supernatural spirit or being who helps witches practice their magic. In medieval Europe, familiars were considered evil by the church, but, in fact, a familiar is simply a guide and a friend. Your familiar could be your cat who sleeps on your bed, a butterfly that unexpectedly comes and sits on your shoulder, or that cute pony in the paddock down the lane.

WHAT YOU NEED

* ✿ **Image of your chosen familiar**
* ✿ **Clear tape/glue**
* ✿ **White candle (to enhance positive protection from your familiar)**

I f you don't already have a pet or animal friend, choose one now from those illustrated here:

Cat, dog, rat, wren, hare, horse, goldfish, snake

Find an image of either your pet or of the animal you have chosen from the list above. If the familiar doesn't yet have a name, give it your own special pet name. Affix the photo or image to the next page and then perform the following spell.

Light the candle and draw a magic circle around the affixed image. Drip a drop of wax onto the image to seal your intention. (If you prefer, you can drip some wax onto a saucer, break it into pieces, and affix one to the image.)

Write around the outside of the circle:

> *My friend will forever bring me grace and calm,*
> *And guard me well to feel no harm.*

Blow out the candle to send the energy of dedication to your familiar, and they will return it back to you whenever you think of them or say their pet name.

Affix photo
or
image here.

BAGUA CHARM FOR HARMONIOUS HOMES

On the opposite page is a feng shui diagram of eight magical symbols, known as the "bagua." When this is aligned with a plan of your home, it tells you where to place various crystals to enhance and attract beneficial energy in corresponding areas of your life.

WHAT YOU NEED

✻ **Tracing paper**
✻ **White quartz crystal**

On a piece of tracing paper, sketch a plan of your home (or you could just start with a plan of your bedroom). Work out which direction your home or room faces and mark the signs of the compass on it.

Under your plan, write down a specific theme in your life which could do with a boost of positive energy. For example, from the basic themes given on the bagua, you might choose "relationships."

Place your plan over the bagua and turn it so that the signs of the compass line up with the direction of the bagua (north to north, etc.).

Find the theme you have chosen on the bagua and look at which area of your home or room this corresponds to.

Say aloud:

I place this crystal to boost positive energy in the [direction] corner of my home.

Activate the crystal's power by placing it in the relevant area of your home.

Place the plan of your home or room over the bagua, aligning
the points of the compass with the direction of the bagua.
Find your theme on the bagua and note which area of your
home/room this corresponds to.

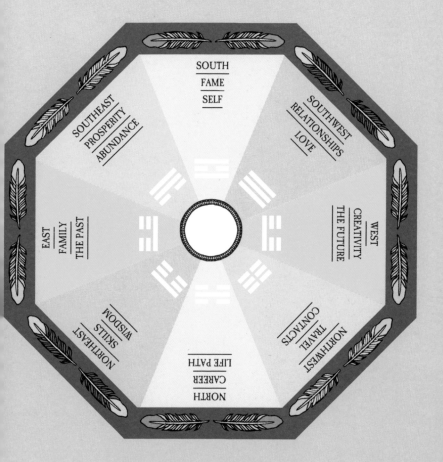

SOUTH
FAME
SELF

SOUTHEAST
PROSPERITY
ABUNDANCE

SOUTHWEST
RELATIONSHIPS
LOVE

EAST
FAMILY
THE PAST

WEST
CREATIVITY
THE FUTURE

NORTHEAST
SKILLS
WISDOM

NORTH
CAREER
LIFE PATH

NORTHWEST
TRAVEL
CONTACTS

*Soon you will find that harmony, peace, and
balance to this area of your life are restored.*

SUCCESS & CREATIVITY

CHAPTER

6

Whatever your definition of success, you are in control of making it happen.

Most people want to be successful, both at work and at home. Some of us may also have spiritual aspirations, romantic goals, or simply a talent that needs to be put to creative use. There are as many types of success as there are individuals, so don't feel you have to be a tycoon, a celebrity, or a politician to succeed.

The word success derives from Latin, meaning "a good result" or "to accomplish a desired result." So if you want to be a successful person, you have to get off your butt and make things happen. Basically that's what magic is—time to create, perform, act, and succeed at your own desired aspirations.

MAGIC MOTIVATOR

There are times when the task in front of you seems harder than mounting a moving broomstick. When motivation is at an all-time low or there aren't enough hours in the day, it's time for a magical pick-me-up! This ancient herb potion will increase your mental prowess, allowing you to take on any task that's thrown your way.

WHAT YOU NEED

* **Dried sage**
  (promotes wisdom)
* **Dried basil**
  (helps to steady the mind)
* **Dill seeds**
  (source of energy)
* **Ground coffee**
  (provides stimulation)
* **Mortar and pestle**
* **Sand**
* **Little bit of water**

Begin by writing a list of tasks you are having trouble with. Then, place the sage, basil, dill seeds, and coffee into the mortar and grind them with the pestle to a fine powder. Add the sand and mix well. Take a pinch of this mixture and add it to a tiny bit of water until it becomes a paste. With your forefinger, paint the paste onto your forehead, between your eyebrows. Gently sprinkle a teaspoonful of the dry mixture over your list of tasks, saying:

Magical mixture of plant and sand
Give my work a helping hand
Grant my mind the power to see
Answers to the question that lies before me.
Both brain and paper are marked by this spell
There's no excuse for me not to do well.
And so I shall begin my wisdom's quest
Knowing my work shall be the best.

Sit quietly for a minute or two, then take your journal outside, being careful not to spill any of the magic mixture from your list of tasks. Then shake the mixture out on the ground, saying a silent prayer of thanks to the powers that be for the help you are about to receive.

List the tasks that are troubling you here:

_____   _____

_____   _____

_____   _____

_____   _____

_____   _____

_____   _____

_____   _____

_____   _____

DEAR
UNIVERSE...

Dreaming of what you can achieve, create, or succeed in is one thing, but you also need to know how to make that dream come true. So, before you do this spell, make sure you have answered the following questions: What is your specific aspiration? What timescale are you hoping for? Is that something you can realistically achieve?

The universe loves to grant us our requests. However, we need to ask and be specific about what we want. Write a letter to the universe, telling it your deepest desires. You can include:

I aspire to . . .
I dream of . . .
I long for . . .
I give out . . .
I take in . . .
I give thanks to . . .
I want to achieve . . .

Read these requests aloud seven times, for seven nights (preferably between a new and full moon). Your success will be guaranteed if you also put these thoughts, desires, and words into action.

CREATIVE THINKING SPELL

In Ancient Egypt, gold was thought to be sent from the sun god, Ra, and has long been a symbol of enrichment — in more ways than one. This spell uses gold and the color red, both powerful enhancements for creativity, whatever you choose to fashion with it.

WHAT YOU NEED

* ✢ **Red candle**
* ✢ **Gold leaf flakes or gold glitter**
* ✢ **Red rose petals (for the growth of passion for your creation)**
* ✢ **A small pouch**

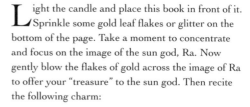

Light the candle and place this book in front of it. Sprinkle some gold leaf flakes or glitter on the bottom of the page. Take a moment to concentrate and focus on the image of the sun god, Ra. Now gently blow the flakes of gold across the image of Ra to offer your "treasure" to the sun god. Then recite the following charm:

> *Seal my quest with rosebud briars,*
> *And weave this spell for my desires.*

Sprinkle the rose petals on the page, then blow out the candle. Leave the rose petals and gold flakes on the open pages overnight. The next morning, put the petals and gold flakes into a pouch and keep them in a secret place for one lunar cycle. This will attract creative thinking in all you do.

Jot down the ways that you express your own creativity.

_____

_____

_____

_____

SUCCESSFUL OPPORTUNITY RITUAL

The medieval mystical symbol known as "caput draconis," meaning "head of the dragon," was often drawn on parchment paper by occult advisors to European kings to ensure they would win their battle or attract favorable trading. The power of this symbol puts you in the center of all action and enables you to take advantage of any opportunity that comes your way.

WHAT YOU NEED

✣ **Green candle**
  (to invoke success)

✣ **Purple candle**
  (to attract opportunity)

E very evening for five nights, light one green and one purple candle, placed on either side of the book, and focus on the symbol on this page for five minutes. Five is the number of profit and will enhance the outcome of this ritual. Focus on the center of the symbol to enable the maximum energy to connect with your own inner power. As you gaze at the symbol say:

My goals are favorable, my success is for me, but I give thanks for all that I receive and the opportunities I take. Whatever I do, this symbol means I do it for myself and for the good of everyone.

Now write the message beneath the symbol to encourage favorable opportunities to come your way. Blow out the candles and, each evening, drip a little wax from each candle onto the symbol to seal your intention.

SUCCESSFUL JOB HUNTING

Runes are ancient Viking symbols that were carved into rocks, stones, and wood, and were used primarily to invoke the power of the gods. For example, the rune "Tyr," also known as "Tiwaz," represents success and victory and was associated with the Norse god Tyr, a mighty warrior, hero, and champion for justice. The rune "Wunjo" is considered to favor good luck, creative work, and professional progress. The rune "Kenaz" invokes clarity about what truly want and what is right for you.

This rune charm will strengthen your resolve and purpose, bringing you success in your search for a new job or career.

As with many "actively seeking something" spells, perform this charm between a new moon and a full moon, and preferably on a Tuesday (named after Tyr in Viking tradition) to invoke the power of this favored god.

Concentrate on the three runes on the page, and focus on your job requirements, career needs, or long-term goal. Is it to get out of a rut or a boring job, or is it to venture forth, take a risk, and try something new? Make sure you know what you are looking for before you do the next part of the charm.

Copy the runes, and below each one write your petitions to invoke their power.

With Tyr
I see my way forward
and know I want to . . .

With Wunjo
I will have
the luck to . . .

With Kenaz
I can see clearly
that I will be . . .

_____   _____   _____

_____   _____   _____

_____   _____   _____

Finally, write:

Thanks to the power of these magical symbols my future will be as I want it to be.

DRAWING DOWN THE MOON'S INSPIRATION

The moon's energy—both invisible and reflective—has been harnessed for thousands of years by magicians and witches. A traditional ritual was to leave a bowl of water or mirror outside on a full moon night to capture its essence. The witch would then gaze at their reflection to draw down or invoke the moon's power from the water or mirror.

Y ou can try the above ritual youself. Or on a full moon night, you can simply focus on the image to the right, as you repeat this spell five times (a mystical power number).

Write the spell in the water in the reflection of the moon:

I draw in the moon's gifts:
of radiance,
of love,
of light,
of personal power,
of ultimate inspirational fulfillment.

You will soon be filled with the light of creative imagination.

DREAMS &
GOALS

CHAPTER

7

Our dreams are personal to us.
Luckily we already have the unique skills
to unlock these dreams inside of us.

The law of attraction basically states that "like attracts like" or, as we say in esoteric and occult circles, "as above, so below." Maybe you've already tried your hand at manifesting money, a new romance, winning a bet, passing an exam, and so on. And maybe you're starting to think this "manifesting" lark isn't all it's cracked up to be. But the only way it will work—like all the magic found in this book—is to truly believe it will. You have to really be able to visualize your desired outcome. Here's a selection of spells to help manifest your desires.

RING ⊕F STⒶNES SPELL

Stone circles, like the Stonehenge and Avebury neolithic monuments in England, were special locations where, during various alignments of the sun, moon, or other celestial bodies, the ancients made magic to please the gods. This circle is where you are going to manifest your first desire. What is your first desire? To believe you are a unique and special person who deserves love and everything you ask for. This is the starting point for getting more of what you want.

WHAT YOU NEED

✿ Scissors

Write each word of the following spell on one of the stones on the next page. It doesn't matter where you start, but work your way around the circle in a clockwise direction. When you have completed the first eleven words, continue going around again until you have circled the stones twice. There are now two words written on each stone. This will bind your spell to the magic circle.

I manifest this desire by binding this stone circle with all my belief, trust, worth, integrity, and my right to be special.

Now choose two words, written on the same stone, that stand out to you. Write them on the stone in the bottom right-hand corner and recite the spell aloud eleven times (eleven is considered by many cultures to be a mystical number, and it represents double energy of the self). Cut out the stone in the corner and place it under your pillow to perpetuate the power of the spell.

Choose two words written on one of the same stones above and write them on the stone to the right.

KNOT SPELL
FOR PROSPERITY

This knot spell will bring you a specific amount of money within a certain time frame. But be realistic. Don't ask for $3,000 by the end of the week, unless you truly believe it's possible.

WHAT YOU NEED

✢ **Two gold candles**

Knot spells bind and focus intentions. Golden threads were used in renaissance tapestries to pull the rich colors into a comprehensive whole. Similarly, the golden threads depicted here will draw the riches of the universe to you.

Know how much you want and the date you want it by—write this down in the space provided at the top of the next page.

Light the two gold candles and place them on either side of your book.

The illustrated gold threads are already braided and knotted. All you have to do at each knot is to write down each line of the charm, saying it aloud as you do so.

With knot one, request is made.
With knot two, amount decreed.
With knot three, desire unfurled.
With knot four, no more, no less.
With knot five, the world be blessed.
With knot six, the gold thread spun.
With knot seven, my will be done.

Date _____   Amount _____

1 _____

2 _____

3 _____

4 _____

5 _____

6 _____

7 _____

*Say this spell aloud every evening within the time frame
you requested to manifest your desired amount.*

FOR BENEFICIAL PROPERTY NEGOTIATION

Some of us are lucky enough to buy our own property, but most of us have to settle for renting or living at home with mom and dad—sometimes it's just too expensive or impractical to do anything else. You, the modern-day witch, may be stuck living somewhere you don't like, but that doesn't mean you have to forever.

WHAT YOU NEED

* ❈ **Piece of citrine** (for good negotiation and manifesting your desire)
* ❈ **Scissors**
* ❈ **Twine/thread**
* ❈ **Small pouch**

P erhaps your goal is to find a great roommate, to move somewhere with a shorter commute, or to buy and sell property. Whatever you want to manifest property-wise, this is the spell to attract it to you.

On the opposite page is a secret cipher. Known as the "witches alphabet" it is still used by Wiccans to write secret messages or spells. First published by the German abbot and cryptologist Johannes Trithemius in the sixteenth century, the script amplifies the power of the citrine when carried with you.

Place your piece of citrine on this page, then write the following spell using the corresponding alphabet. Copy the spell onto the strip at the side of the next page, cut it out, wrap it around the piece of citrine, and tie it together with twine or thread. Place it in a pouch, and carry it everywhere you go to attract beneficial property negotiations.

> *With these words I charge this stone*
> *To bring me soon my perfect home.*

a		b		c		d	
e		f		g		h	
i,j		k		l		m	
n		o		p		q	
r		s		t		u,v	
w		x		y		z	

Translate the spell using the witches alphabet.
Copy it onto the strip at the side of the page.
Cut the strip out and wrap it around the citrine.

GOOD FORTUNE CHARM

When things are going right for everyone else, they may seem to be going wrong for you, and vice versa. But a change of fortune—in the right direction— is always welcome.

In feng shui, the so-called "lucky bamboo" plant has long been the Chinese symbol for fortune and self-empowerment. The number of bamboo stalks determines the kind of energy the plant attracts into your home and life. The more stalks, the greater the good fortune. So for good fortune, keep a plant with at least nine stalks, as this number is highly auspicious.

Here's an illustration of a nine-stalk lucky bamboo. Along each stalk, write a word that sums up one of your desires. Soon these things will come to you, especially if you incorporate a real plant in your home and place it in a southern or southeastern part of a room. Good luck!

Along each stalk, write a word that sums up one of your desires.

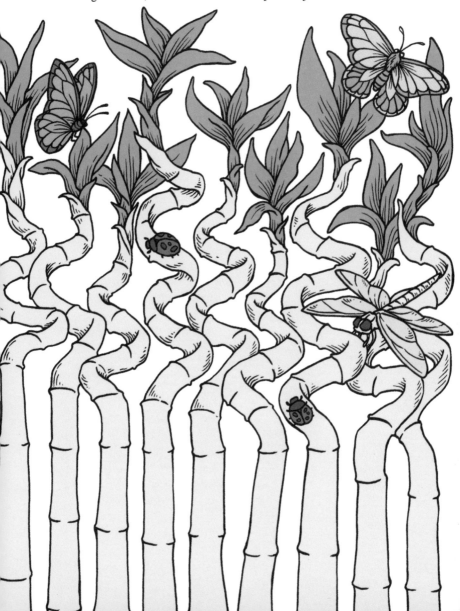

MANIFEST SPIRITUAL ENLIGHTENMENT

Spiritual enlightenment is experienced in many different ways. You might suddenly realize that you and the universe are one. Or you might have an epiphany moment, when everything falls into place, and you feel you are exactly where you are meant to be in life. It can be an illuminating experience of awe, an "a-ha" moment, or simply a deep sensation of peace.

WHAT YOU NEED

✿ **Colored pens/pencils**

If you would like to be enlightened in some way, follow in the path of the Buddha who, according to legend, left his footprint on the stone floor on which he stepped the moment after his own enlightenment.

Depictions of this print, known as a "buddhapada," are found in ancient Buddhist temples. Inside the outline of the footprint are three other auspicious Buddhist symbols: the Dharma Wheel (top), the Three Jewels (center), and the Lotus (bottom).

Starting from the little toe, write the letters of your name on each toe. For names with more than five letters, write any additional letters under the first letters. For example, for the name "Miranda," the "D" would be written under the "M" of the little toe.

Next, color the symbols as desired. Then write the following spell in the path of footsteps around the illustration:

Every step I take on the pathway to enlightenment or for personal life-changing revelation will be because I believe in the unity of All and the potential within myself to make my own footprint in stone. Bless All who Know the Way.

On each toe, write the letters of your name, color in the symbols, and write the spell in the path of footsteps.

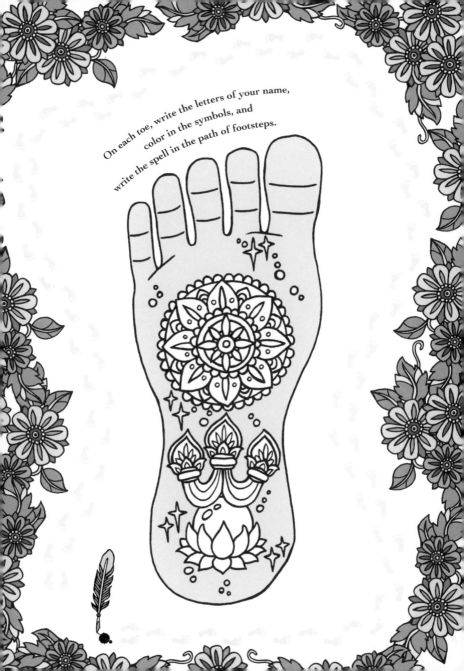

FRIENDSHIP & MENTORS

CHAPTER

8

True friends are priceless, so treat them as you would a treasure chest of beautiful things.

The relationship between friends is a truly magical one. Unlike family, we seek out these kindred spirits who completely get us, appreciate our twisted sense of humor, and encourage us to be our best selves. And, when we find these bewitching creatures, we tend to hold on tight. Sometimes friendship takes a back seat—boyfriends take precedence, careers come first, or sisterhoods simply don't work out. Be sure to take some time to reprioritize your friendships. Decide whether you want to widen your social circle, banish bad vibes, or move existing friendships onto a closer, more supportive basis.

CHAMOMILE CALMER

When friends are at each other's throats it can feel like the sisterhood is splitting apart. Use your witchy wisdom to bring the coven back together with a calming cup of chamomile, which has been used for centuries for healing.

WHAT YOU NEED

* ✿ Chamomile flowers (1¼ oz. (35g) dried or 2¾ oz. (77g) fresh)
* ✿ Teapot
* ✿ Bowl
* ✿ Large plant pot
* ✿ Soil
* ✿ Chamomile plants or cuttings

To make a chamomile infusion, add the dried or fresh chamomile flowers to 17 fl oz. (500ml) of boiling water, in a teapot, and leave to infuse for around 10 minutes. Using a strainer, pour yourself a cup to drink, and then strain the rest into a bowl and leave it to cool. While it is cooling, fill the pot with soil, and plant a chamomile. Bring the rift between your friends to mind and chant this rhyme as you work:

Show me the charm of flowers,
Sing me the spell of peace.

When you have finished, wash your hands in the warm infusion, then water the plants with it. As you do so, make a wish that their friendship will be refreshed and grow stronger with the plant.

Write down the reasons for the discord between your friends. Then cross all these out with a thick line, so that they are no more.

_____

_____

_____

_____

_____

_____

Then write the names of your friends entwined with each other, to bring them back together.

RECONCILIATION SPELL

According to an old Japanese legend, the Milky Way separated two lovers, the stars Orihime and Hikoboshi. Only on the seventh day of the seventh lunar month were they allowed to meet. The Star Festival, the Tanabata, is celebrated on this day in Japan.

During the festival, people write their wish for happy reunions or joyful reconciliations on scraps of colored paper. The paper is tied to bamboo sticks and set afloat on the river as an offering to the two star deities. This similar ritual will bring you happy reunions with those pals you've not seen for some time or wish to get close to again.

Write the names of people you want to be reconciled or reunited with on one of the paper flags shown here. Seven nights later or during a full moon night (if that comes first), write the following charm:

Orihime and Hikoboshi twinkle bright
To bring us close again one night.

Very soon, you and a pal will be happily reunited.

BESTIE BOUQUET

We know we can always rely on some special friends for support, a spirit of adventure, or just a good laugh. So keep these relationships sweet with this ritual that will bring you both mutual respect and joyful times.

Flowers were believed to express various sentiments when given as a gift. Below is a list of flowers with their traditional symbolic meanings. Choose a flower that reminds you of a pal you want to be in your bestie bouquet. (You don't have to have nine friends, maybe just a few, or even one for now—you can always add to the bouquet as time goes on.)

Forget-me-not — They won't let you forget you're special
Chamomile — Tolerant, charming, patient
Daisy — Optimistic, fun, a laugh
Lilac — Youthful, free-spirited
Pansy — Thoughtful, caring, spiritual
Lavender — Devoted, faithful
Iris — Chatty, gives great advice
Hollyhock — Ambitious, driven
Cherry blossom — Trustworthy, reliable

Color in the appropriate flower/s and write your friend's name underneath the flower.

Then seal the intention by writing this incantation:

These flowers will bring me friendships true,
Each one new joy for me and you.

WHAT YOU NEED

✿ **Colored pens/pencils**

Lilac for my friend: _____

Hollyhock for my friend: _____

Color in the flowers and write your friends' names underneath.

Forget-me-not for my friend:

Chamomile for my friend:

Daisy for my friend:

Pansy for my friend:

Lavender for my friend:

Iris for my friend:

Cherry blossom for my friend:

WHO CAN YOU TRUST RITUAL

Social media doesn't exactly make it easy to keep quiet about much these days. But if you want to confide in someone, then this ritual will sort out who can be trusted with your secrets.

WHAT YOU NEED

* **Small tea light candles (one for each friend you want to check out)**
* **Pin or needle**
* **Colored pens/ pencils**

Take the tea light out of its metal case, and carve the name of your pal (with a pin or needle) around the side of the candle—make sure the wick is upright and the candle is on a flat surface. Light the candle, and watch how it burns for a few minutes.

• If it burns true and the flame is still, your pal is completely trustworthy.

• If it flickers erratically on and off, your friend can be a bit of a gossip.

• If it goes out or flickers constantly, then don't trust this friend!

On the next page, write the names of the friends you can trust on the side of the candles and color them in. Use colors that make you feel joyful about and grateful for your pals. Now you can safely tell them your secrets.

Write the names of the friends you can trust on
the side of the candles and color the candles.

POSITIVE MENTORS MANDALA

Apart from new friends, we also sometimes need people to guide us, give us wise advice, teach us something new, or get us through the university of life. If you know what kind of mentor, guru, or advisor you need right now, then use this ancient ritual to draw this person into your life.

WHAT YOU NEED

* Colored pens/pencils
* Candle

The mandala (Sanscrit word meaning "circle") is a spiritual and meditational device used in Hinduism and Buddhism. Rich in symbolism, mandalas represent the entire universe or cosmos. The ancient Aztec "sunstone" is now considered to be a form of ritual mandala.

In the center of the mandala, write down the kind of mentor you are looking for. Maybe you need career advice, a wellness motivator, a creative guru, or just someone with fresh perspective. Color the mandala in any way you like. As you color, meditate on your desire; concentrate and focus on bringing the person with the qualities you seek into your life.

Write the kind of mentor you are seeking in the middle of the mandala.
Color the mandala, focusing on your desire to bring this person into your life.

Once you have finished, light a candle, and thank the universe for its
help, as it's about to send you a powerful ally.

BANISH BAD VIBES SPELL

Pals can get rattled about all kinds of things. They can be envious of our job, our love life, or just wish they had flowing locks like ours. Work colleagues get secretly heated because we got a heads-up on a deal, or jealous about our ability to charm the boss. In fact, bad energy surrounds us everywhere, and although we can protect ourselves from it by carrying or wearing crystals, we sometimes need to banish it completely.

WHAT YOU NEED
- **White tea light candle**
- **Rose petals**
- **Ylang ylang oil**

This spell, like all banishing spells, should be performed during a waning moon period.

Sprinkle some rose petals around the base of the candle and drizzle a few drops of ylang ylang oil onto the candle and the petals. Now light the candle and gaze into the flame while you repeat the following:

This candle I burn to banish bad thoughts.
This candle I burn to reverse any curse.
This candle I burn to turn wrong to good.
This candle will burn away all that it should.

If you don't have the oil or rose petals, you can simply light a white candle and focus on that while you repeat the spell. But the spell will be much more powerful if you can use the ingredients too.

Write down the intention behind this spell: What bad vibes are you dealing with now?

Drizzle a few drops of oil in this corner while you repeat the spell. Cut off the spell-infused corner of your book and keep it in your pocket. By the next full moon you will find negative vibes are replaced with peaceful ones.

WHAT YOU NEED

✿ Gold pen
✿ Piece of rose quartz crystal

GOOD VIBES FOR A FAR-AWAY PAL

Send benevolent, supportive, or healing energy to a far-away friend. They may be on the other side of the globe or live in another city. Whatever the case, this ritual will send your love and healing energy to whoever has need of it.

Mark the approximate location of your friend's whereabouts on the map and write their name and your wish for them next to it. Place the crystal over their name. Write the spell in gold pen, and then repeat aloud.

> *This spell is writ with lines of gold,*
> *A time for love to be so bold,*
> *So cross the river or the sands,*
> *To heal with crystals in your hands.*

Now blow gently on the crystal and the world map, and imagine yourself blowing a gale of kisses in the direction of your friend.

Mark the location of your
friend on the map and write
their name and your wish
for them next to it.

N
W   E
S

Positive, healing, or supportive energy will be winging its way to your friend's door.

INDEX

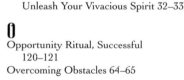

CREDITS

I would like to thank Quarto and everyone who helped produce this book
to make its magic real. My appreciation goes especially to my "coven-mates,"
Kate Kirby, Victoria Lyle, Karin Skånberg, Rachel Urquhart, and not forgetting
my agent, Chelsey Fox.

I wish also to express my gratitude to my familiars and family for experiencing
and delighting in the spells created for this journal. My special thanks go to my
daughter, Jess, for her magical support.